Minx Is Missing

Published by Write Impression Ltd.
Copyright 2022 Feline Fix & Hannah Walker
Photographs by Jacqui Graham

ALL RIGHTS RESERVED
No part of this publication may be reproduced, stored in a retrieval system transmitted in any form or by any means, electronic, mechanical, photocopying, recording or otherwise, without prior written permission from the publisher.

ISBN 978-0-473-65888-5

Minx is who I am. I'm big and bold and strong.
I'm sorry about the things that I did wrong.

I did not mean to steal poor Archie's food,

But, boy, it tasted really good.

I'm boisterous and frisky,
And sometimes a little rough,
But all I want to do is play,

And I don't always know when
Archie's had enough.

So, his people came one day
And took me far away.

They drove me up a steep and curving street.
I enjoyed the view from their back seat.

On and on we went.
No one told me what it meant.

Then they stopped, opened the door,
And invited me out to go and explore.

Off they drove without me, in haste.
I had no idea what I would face?

So, I sat down beside a tree for a wash.
They had been mean to me: really quite harsh.

I would have to find my own way back,
But by now it was almost pitch black.
I knew in the morning there would be light,
But it was cold and scary on that dark night.

I managed to find a place to sleep
On Paekak' Hill amongst the sheep.

A big storm came in the morning,
Thunder and lightning, wind and rain.
To me it was all very wild and exciting,
But to Archie it would not have been the same.
He was afraid of bangs and crashes,
And hated those bright, lightning flashes.

When cars drive past his house,
He hides away like a mouse.
Barking dogs make him very scared,
So, for this storm, he'd be quite unprepared.
He would have no clue what to do.
I hadn't given it much thought before,
But perhaps he had been afraid of me too?
I'd have to change my ways, for sure!
Not all cats are bold like me,
Some are quite timid, you see?

**Archie did not like being afraid,
Of the rough and tumble games that I played.**

Yes, my behaviour had been unkind.
I thought it over and made up my mind.

I would be a lot more careful,
With others who are quite fearful.

Archie will know that he can depend,
On me as his kind and gentle best friend.

I was still lost and all alone,
Missing my warm and comfy home,
But I knew my family would soon find me,
Because Hannah, Damien, Lydia and Bradley,
All love me very dearly.

My friend Archie is truly unfortunate:
His people are not so compassionate.

I wandered about for a while,
Till I found a man with a kind, gentle smile.

He took me in, out of the cold and rain.
It wasn't my home, but I couldn't complain.

Out there, my family was searching,
While on a soft couch I was perching.

I was cozy and warm,
And safe from the storm.

I had lots of good food to eat,
But my soul felt incomplete.

I was missing my home and my friends,
And, this is how the story ends:

Just as I knew they would,
My family did all that they could.

They discovered where I was staying,
And without any further delaying,
They came to get me and took me home:
Never again would I be forced to roam.

The Background to Minx's Story

I'm Hannah Walker. When we were still at university sharing a flat, my partner and I adopted Minx. He was our first "baby," and, as such, we love him dearly. Over the years, he has sailed through many of life's changes with us. He has had to deal with puppies, real babies and a new kitten, but he's managed all of them with grace, taking everything in his stride.

Minx is a big 8-year-old boy, weighing in at around 6 kilograms. He isn't overweight: he's tall and powerfully built, and sometimes unaware of his own strength. He's also very confident and curious about everything. He knows his mind and can be very assertive. One of our neighbours joked about how Minx guards their doggy door and won't let their dog outside. Despite his size and assertiveness, Minx is a real lovebug. He insists on sleeping under the blankets with us and loves to cuddle.

On May 4th, 2022, Minx didn't come home. This was unusual. When he had still not returned two days later, we began posting on social media and putting flyers in all the mailboxes on our street. Four days in, I got a text from an anonymous number saying that they knew what had become of Minx. They said their flatmate was annoyed that Minx had been bullying their cat, so they trapped him and took him to Paekakariki Hill and dumped him there.

On May 10th, I set up a Facebook page to enlist the community's help to bring Minx home. We were blown away by the support we received, and we'd like to thank every one of you from the bottom of our hearts. Forgotten Felines Foundation gave us great advice, supplied traps and trail cams to monitor activity at the feeding stations we set up, and we had unstinting help from volunteers who monitored and maintained them. Our volunteers did flyer drops, bushwhacked Paekakariki Hill in the foulest of weather, and shared Facebook posts far and wide.

We personally went up that hill at least three times a week while Minx was missing. On the first evening after I had found out what had happened to him, I ran into Helen who had already been there for an hour, calling his name from the road. She was there pretty much every day, knocking on doors, talking to residents, playing recordings of me calling him, and the like. This angel didn't know me or Minx – she was simply a decent human being helping out of the goodness of her heart. I was moved to tears by Helen's kindness.

Another incredible person is my closest friend, Jacqui. Within ten minutes of me telling her the story, she was already in touch with Forgotten Felines Foundation, securing a feeding station and arranging for someone to collect it. She went to the feeding station whenever I couldn't, and she drove me to the station at 10PM on the night of Minx's first sighting. I wouldn't have been able to get through the ordeal without her.

After Minx had been gone for a week, we took the decision to file a police report. We were advised to go softly at first so as to let the whistleblower come forward of their own accord and to not lose that opportunity. Nothing came of it, however, and we were forced to escalate. Despite all our efforts, we didn't get a lot of support from this quarter, all while Minx was alone and exposed to the worst of Wellington's wintry weather. My heart broke to think that he was out there alone, unprotected, cold and hungry in those conditions, and I wondered often how anyone could have been so wantonly cruel.

Expenses were mounting when we realised we were in for a long haul. We set up a Give-a-Little appeal to help defray the costs of printing flyers, additional feeding stations, SD cards for the trail cams, care and support of other cats we caught, as well as reimbursing our volunteers for their petrol. Once again, we were overwhelmed by community support. Wherever we had potential sightings, we set traps, catching four other kitties in the process. Three of them were reunited with their owners, while one was rehomed after weeks of trying to locate his people.

We continued like this for months. I was starting to despair, wondering if we would ever have Minx back home again. Then, in the early morning of Monday, July 25th, came the call I had been longing for. Someone had Minx! Apparently, about a month earlier, they had seen a Tabby in their garden, and had started feeding him. He was nervous and skittish at first, but eventually plucked up the courage to walk in and start sleeping on their bed! Then, by chance, they saw a three-month-old Facebook post and realised the "wild" cat was actually Minx. The kind people were sad to say goodbye to him but felt better about it when they saw how much we had been missing him. Within half an hour of their message, our Minx was finally home!

We think that Minx's experience is a good lesson, and that's why we're telling the story. He's not a bully: he's just a big, boisterous cat with a healthy self-esteem. By contrast, the people who took and dumped him exhibited not only bullying, but cowardly behaviour. If Minx had made their cat feel threatened, a simple word to us would have been enough for us to remedy the situation. Now that he's back with us, we are keeping him indoors and have built a catio to keep him happily confined.

With this simple children's story, we hope to encourage youngsters to reflect on their own behaviour. More often than not, children seen as bullies are indeed well-meaning, but have not been sensitised about how their behaviour affects others.

If the people who stole Minx had had this childhood foundation, they might not have trapped and dumped him so cruelly.

We are sympathetic to children and adults who are victims of bullying, and we hope that Minx's story might help to change the outlook of children who aren't aware of their own strength and the adverse effects of their assertiveness.

Profits from the book go to Feline Fix, a wonderful organisation which subsidises the de-sexing of cats, providing financial assistance to Rescue Organisations and individuals for this purpose.

Hannah Walker, August 2022

Photographs of Minx by Jacqui Graham
facebook.com/JacquelineIrisPhotography
Website: jacquelineiris.co.nz

Feline Fix is a Kapiti-based charity working in the community to help spay and neuter cats. We assist families to de-sex their pets and encourage responsible pet ownership. We 'grin like Cheshire cats' at the thought of how many animal lives have been saved through de-sexing. In just three years, more than 400 cats have been spayed and neutered, and a large number of unwanted kittens has been re-homed through our friends in animal rescue. It's all about teamwork. Together, we strive to prevent unwanted litters. The horror of kittens having kittens is utterly preventable, and it's vital to de-sex early. This costs money. The proceeds of this book will help us achieve even more.

It may have been a 'furry-tail' ending for Minx, but not all cats are so lucky. The reason he was discarded like a piece of trash disgusts us beyond words, but now he's back home with his loving family and has become a symbol of what is good in our community. Everyone who rallied to find him never gave up hope. From something so evil has come something good. The team who searched for Minx brought awareness to the plight of many cats living in the wild: feral, unloved, lost and alone. Many are rescued by angels, and the work continues to help even more. All of this comes down to people not de-sexing their pets. Feline Fix would like to be the ambulance at the top of the cliff, preventing unwanted litters. Please do not litter in New Zealand –

de-sex your critter!

We hope you enjoy the book – 'the Good, the Bad and the Cuddly' – and thank you for supporting all cats by purchasing a copy. Together, we can do more to save lives. There are far too many kittens being born, and not enough loving forever homes for them.

Enjoy Jacqui's lovely photos of Minx,

    Annette Buckley

If you enjoyed Minx's story, you may enjoy one of my other books. Profits from these books support cats in need and cat charities.

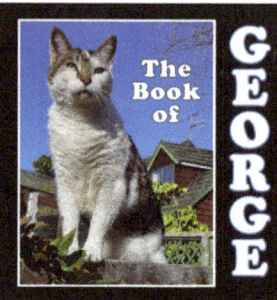

You can reach me by email:

cats@deanes.co.nz

Or connect with me on Facebook:

facebook.com/TheNotSoCrazyCatLady

Linda Deane

www.ingramcontent.com/pod-product-compliance
Lightning Source LLC
Chambersburg PA
CBHW062044290426
44109CB00026B/2724